WIZOO Quick Start

Mark Wherry

Cubase SX

Wise Publications
in association with (:wizoo:)

Exclusive distributors:
Music Sales Limited
8/9 Frith Street, London W1D 3JB, England.

Music Sales Pty Limited
120 Rothschild Avenue, Rosebery, NSW 2018, Australia.

Author: Mark Wherry.
Publisher: Peter Gorges.

Cover art: Design Box, Ravensberg, Germany.
Editor: Reinhard Schmitz.
Interior design and layout: Uwe Senkler.

Copyright © 2002 Wizoo Publishing GmbH, Bremen, Germany.

Order No. AM976019
ISBN 0-7119-9755-1

Printed in the United Kingdom.

www.musicsales.com

Welcome

Like all Wizoo Quick Starts, this book is designed to help you get a handle on the topic as quickly and easily as possible. To this end, the Quick Starts are written in concise, easy-to-understand language and include CD-ROMs that provide tutorial materials for hands-on experience.

This book is your personal guide to becoming a Cubase SX master and is basically split into two sections. First of all we'll look at setting up Cubase SX to work in harmony with your computer's audio and MIDI hardware, before taking a guided tour of the most common windows and learning some basic mixing skills.

In the second part of the book, you'll be recording a song from scratch, learning how to program a drum part, and finally, mastering a finished song that can be written to an audio CD, or stored as an MP3 file to share with others on the Internet. You'll also find a couple of pages filled with troubleshooting tips and the answers to frequently asked questions.

Here's hoping you enjoy reading, listening, and trying things out. Above all, I wish you lots of success learning the ropes!

Peter Gorges, Publisher

Table of Contents

Table of Contents

Getting Started

Before we can start making music with Cubase SX, it's important to make sure that everything's configured to work correctly with your *audio* and *MIDI* hardware.

❖ Open the Device Setup window by selecting "Devices > Device Setup."

The Device Setup window contains all the settings that tell Cubase how to interact with your computer's hardware, whether it's MIDI and audio, or more advanced configurations like video, control surfaces and networking with other computers running Cubase (using what's known as the VST System Link).

The concept of *Digital Audio* is very easy to understand. A recording made from the real world with a microphone, guitar and so on, is stored as digital audio data on your computer. It contains the exact sound you hear and is commonly stored as Wave (∗.WAV) files. The best example of digital audio is a CD.

MIDI (Musical Instrument Digital Interface) data records the blueprints for a musical performance, as opposed to audio data where the actual sound is recorded. MIDI information consists of different events that describe the music, such as 'play note C4,' 'change the volume level to 40,' and so on.

MIDI

MIDI connections are relatively easy to deal with since Cubase should automatically recognize and use any MIDI hardware you have installed on your computer.

If you want to know more about MIDI technology, check out the "MIDI" Quick Start.

Testing the MIDI Input

If you have a MIDI keyboard hooked up to your computer (either directly via USB, or using an additional MIDI interface), there's a very simply way to check that it's communicating with Cubase.

In order to connect MIDI equipment (like a keyboard or sound module) to your computer, you need an additional MIDI interface. Often, this will be via a simple lead that connects to your joystick port and provides a basic MIDI input and output port.

1 If you can't see the Transport Panel, temporarily close the Device Setup window.

2 Open the Transport Panel by selecting "Transport > Transport Panel" or by pressing F2.

3 The MIDI In indictor should light up (red) when you play notes on your keyboard.

You can also connect more advanced MIDI interfaces to your computer, and these usually work with your USB port. Certain MIDI keyboards, like those developed by MIDIMan and Evolution, also contain a MIDI interface, so the keyboard connects directly to your computer over a single USB lead. In this case, you won't have to worry about MIDI connections.

Nothing's Happening!

You can see the complete list of MIDI inputs and outputs available to Cubase by selecting "Windows MIDI" from the Devices list. If your MIDI keyboard (or interface) isn't on the list, you'll need to try reinstalling it, rebooting your computer and running Cubase again. If there's still no input and it doesn't appear in the "Windows MIDI" panel, consult the manual or speak to the manufacturer.

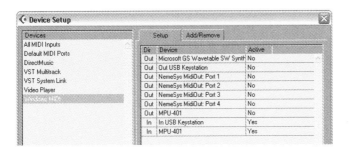

The Windows MIDI panel shows all the MIDI input (and output) ports available to Windows. Notice the inputs available on my system: a joystick-to-MIDI adaptor ("MPU-401") and a USB MIDI keyboard ("In USB Keystation").

What about MIDI Output?

In order to hear the notes you play on a MIDI keyboard, or those recorded in a song you're playing back, you need to have a MIDI sound source. This might be the built-in sounds on your keyboard, for example, or perhaps an external MIDI sound module you've connected. However, in this guide we'll be using VST instruments that create a MIDI sound source in software, without needing any extra equipment.

The data Cubase sends to a MIDI sound source when you play notes on a MIDI keyboard, or play a recorded song, is known as MIDI output.

Audio

Audio hardware can be slightly more tricky to setup because there are many extra considerations depending on whether you've bought extra hardware or are using the internal audio hardware that came with your computer—the basic headphone and mic jacks, for example.

To configure your audio hardware in Cubase:

1 Open the Device Setup window. (Quick reminder: select "Devices > Device Setup.")

2 Select "VST Multitrack" from the list of devices.

ASIO (Audio Streaming Input Output) is a Steinberg technology for getting audio into and out of the computer as efficiently as possible.

An *ASIO driver* is a small piece of software that acts as a bridge between your audio hardware and software. If you're buying new audio hardware, always check for the availability of ASIO drivers to ensure compatibility with Cubase.

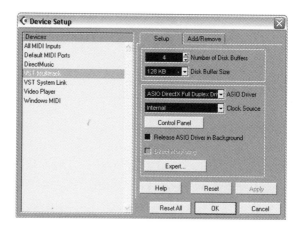

Working with Additional Audio Hardware

If you have additional audio hardware connected to your computer as an internal PCI card, or maybe via a USB or FireWire interface, it probably installed a dedicated *ASIO driver* for Cubase when you loaded the CD-ROM that came with the device. You should be able to choose this driver by clicking on the ASIO Driver pop-up menu.

I Don't Have Any Extra Audio Hardware

If you don't have any additional audio hardware, select "ASIO DirectX Full Duplex Driver" as your ASIO driver.

If you hear unpleasant noises when you start working with Cubase (while a song is playing, for example), try changing the ASIO driver to "ASIO Multimedia Driver." Although not quite as efficient, it tends to be more compatible than the DirectX driver.

Latency Lowdown

Latency is the amount of time it takes to hear the result of an action you carry out. This means that if you were using a software instrument, where the sound is generated by the computer, the latency is the time it takes for you to hear the sound after pressing a key on your MIDI keyboard.

If you're recording audio into Cubase, a high latency will mean that you hear what you're recording as much as a second after playing it. And if you're starting to think this is all a joke, welcome to the wonderful world of latency.

However, there are many ways to get around the issue of latency, and we'll look at these more closely when we get to the relevant sections in this guide.

An extra audio card or USB/FireWire device that comes with its own dedicated ASIO drivers is usually capable of lower latencies than the standard audio hardware that comes with your computer.

About Disk Buffer Settings

If you're the sort of person who's curious about every little detail, you'll have noticed the settings for Disk Buffers in the VST Multitrack panel.

With more and larger-sized disk *buffers*, you'll get smoother results when playing and recording audio files because less demand is placed on the processor for disk access. However, the latency also increases when you increase these values, so it becomes something of a balancing act.

> Rule of thumb: Always leave these settings with their default values to start with. If you start to experience 'glitches' during the playback and recording of audio files, try increasing these values to see if you can get smoother performance.

A *buffer* is an amount of memory used as an intermediate stage when data is being moved around the computer. In Cubase, buffers are used when reading data from the hard disk during playback, and also when writing data to the hard disk during recording, for example.

Buffer Sizes on Your Audio Hardware

In the same way that buffers are used by Cubase when transferring audio to and from your hard drive, they are also used to transfer audio to and from your soundcard.

The settings for buffer sizes on your audio hardware can usually be configured in the ASIO driver's control panel.

❖ Click the Control Panel button in the VST Multitrack panel of the Device Setup window.

Although the control panel that appears will be specific to the hardware you're using, look for references to buffer size and latency. As an example, the control panel for users running the ASIO DirectX Full Duplex Driver is illustrated below.

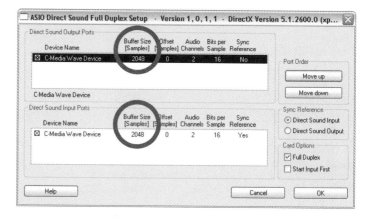

By lowering the buffer size values, you can dramatically reduce the latency of your audio hardware. However, it's important to remember that smaller buffer sizes also place more demand on your processor, so start with the lowest buffer size your hardware supports (128 or 256 are usually good starting points) and work backwards until there are no apparent audio glitches.

A Guided Tour

2

Now that your MIDI and audio hardware is properly configured, it's time to start looking at the more enjoyable aspects of Cubase. And there's no better way of doing this than with the aid of a demo song.

1 Copy the Demo Song folder from the CD-ROM to a convenient location on your computer's hard drive.

2 In Cubase, select "File > Open," choose Demo Song > Demo Song.cpr in the file selector, and click Open.

Having a separate hard drive for audio work is a great idea, but most computer hard drives are fast enough to cope with both audio and system files when you're getting started.

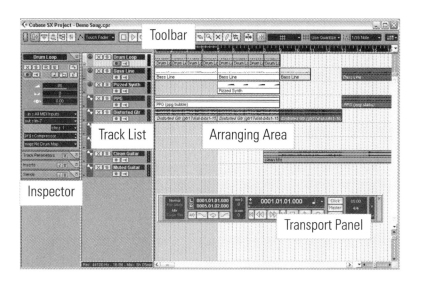

Two key elements in Cubase are the Project window, where the song is constructed, and the Transport Panel, which provides the controls for playing and recording the song.

The Project window is split into four sections: the toolbar, the track list, the Inspector, and the arranging area.

The Project Window

Every Cubase song is constructed in a Project window, and it's even possible to open many Project windows simultaneously. The currently active Project window is illustrated by the "active" light in the top left-hand corner of the window.

One of the most important aspects of the Project window is the track list, which is the list of tracks making up your song. Generally speaking, each track provides the space to record one instrument, and Cubase supports many different track types for recording different kinds of musical information. For example, you'll notice both audio and MIDI tracks on the demo song's Project window.

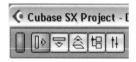

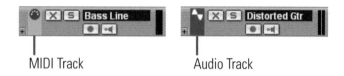

MIDI Track   Audio Track

An *event* is a single block of audio. A *part* is a collection of events, or a single block of MIDI data.

The main arranging area is where your music is displayed as *parts* and *events*, which are represented by rectangular blocks. Notice how the parts and events line up with the tracks on the track list, and also how they're displayed along a time ruler, which usually shows the time duration of the song in terms of bars and beats.

If you can't see the Inspector (or if you ever want to hide the Inspector to save screen space), use the Hide/Show Inspector button on the Project window's toolbar.

To the left of the track list is the Inspector, which presents a variety of settings for the currently selected track.

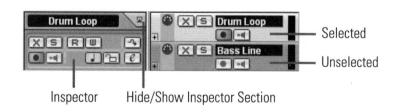

Selected

Unselected

Inspector   Hide/Show Inspector Section

The currently selected track is highlighted on the Project window, and the top line of the Inspector shows the name of the track whose settings will be changed. To select a track on the Project window, simply click it.

The Transport Panel

Among other things, the Transport Panel provides the basic controls to play and record your song, and takes the familiar visual appearance of traditional tape machines.

You can hide and show the Transport Panel by pressing F2 or by selecting "Transport > Transport Panel."

Try clicking the Play button to hear a couple of bars of the demo song, and then click the Stop button.

> If you hear a metronome click, you can disable this by deactivating the Click button on the Transport Panel, or by pressing C.

The Song Position Pointer

When the song plays, you'll notice a line moving across the Project window to indicate the current playback position. This line is known as the Project Cursor. When Cubase is stopped, the location of the Project Cursor shows where Cubase will start from when you press the Play button again.

Time Ruler

Song Position Pointer

To make the Project Cursor jump to a new location, click in the lower part of the time ruler at the relevant place. When Cubase is stopped, a particularly neat trick is to double-click in the lower part of the time ruler, which will start playback at the point you double-clicked.

Using Shortcuts for Transport Controls

Learning the keyboard shortcuts for common transport controls can really accelerate your Cubase work.

Notice that there are dupli-cate Play and Stop buttons on the Project window's toolbar.

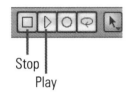

Stop
Play

❖ To play the song, press enter on the numeric keypad.

❖ To stop the song, press ⓪ on the numeric keypad.

❖ Pressing the Stop key again will move the Project Cursor back to the position you previously played the song from.

❖ To move the Project Cursor back to the beginning of the song (or "return to zero," as they say), press the . key on the numeric keypad.

Numbering the Bars and Beats

Cubase displays musical time locations in bars and beats as a four figure number, which shows (from left to right) bars, quarter notes, sixteenth notes and ticks. For example, the current song playback position is given in this format on the Transport Panel.

bars   sixteenth notes

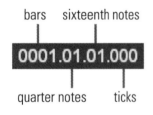

0001.01.01.000

quarter notes   ticks

The bar number is fairly straight forward, showing the number of the bar. Quarter notes reflect the number of quarter notes in the time signature, so the sequence for a bar in 4/4 time would be: 1.1.1.0 > 1.2.1.0 > 1.3.1.0 > 1.4.1.0 > 2.1.1.0. The sixteenth notes divide the quarter notes into four, so the sequence for a quarter note would be: 1.1.1.0 > 1.1.2.0 > 1.1.3.0 > 1.1.4.0 > 1.2.1.0. Ticks divide the bar even further into thousands of tiny beats, although we won't need this level of precision just now.

If all this seems a little complicated, don't worry—it will become clearer as we work through the next sections.

Locators and Cycling

In addition to the Project Cursor, you can also set the location of various markers on the time ruler—the first two markers are known as the left and right locators. These have many uses in Cubase, including setting the boundaries for cycle playback mode.

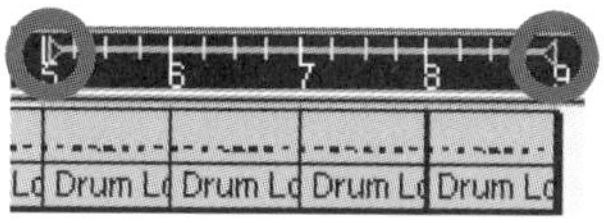

the left and right locators

Let's say we want to set the left locator to bar 5 and the right locator to bar 9. Although there are many ways of doing this, the simplest is just to drag in the upper half of the time ruler from bars 5 to 9.

As you move the mouse over the upper part of the time ruler (in order to drag out the new locator positions), the mouse cursor should change to a pencil symbol.

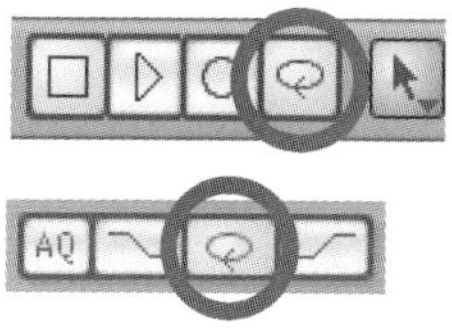

❖ To activate cycle mode, click the cycle button on the Transport Panel (or Project window), or press [/] on the numeric keypad.

So long as the Project Cursor is inside the left and right locators while the song is playing, Cubase will now play the four bar region between bars 5 and 9 indefinitely until the song is stopped, or the Project Cursor is moved outside the locators.

The Track Mixer

In addition to the Project window and Transport Panel, there's a third window you'll probably spend a fair amount of time staring at: the Track Mixer.

❖ To open the Track Mixer, press [F3] or select "Devices > Track Mixer."

The Track Mixer can be configured to show many different views.

The Track Mixer mimics the look of a conventional hardware mixing console, and allows you to control the volume, panning, and various other track-type-specific parameters. When you open the Track Mixer, you'll notice that the order the tracks appear (from left to right) is exactly the same order as they're listed (from top to bottom) on the Project window.

The MIDI Editors

So far, we've looked at the windows used for arranging, transport control and mixing, but none of these provide a way of taking a closer look at the actual music being played. For this, Cubase provides various editor windows for both audio and MIDI information, and the appropriate editor is always opened when you double-click a part or event on the Project window.

❖ Double-click the Bass Line part at the beginning of the song.

The Bass Line part is opened in the default MIDI editor, which is usually the Key editor.

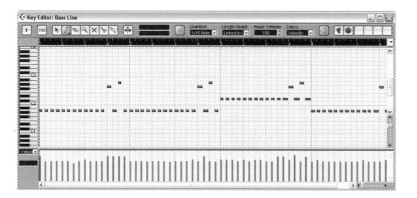

The Key editor shows a pitch/duration view (often called a piano roll) of every note in the selected part.

❖ Close the Key editor.

Cubase has a variety of editors to show your MIDI data in different ways. For example, if you're more comfortable reading traditional music notation, you could view the same Bass Line part with the Score editor.

1 Select the part you want to open, in this case the Bass Line part at the beginning of the song.

2 Select "MIDI > Open Score Editor" or press ctrl R.

3 By default, you'll notice that the treble clef is chosen and notes are written mostly off the stave with many ledger lines. Since this is a bass part, we really want it to be displayed with the bass clef.

4 To change the clef for the whole part, simply double-click the clef at bar one.

5 Choose the bass clef with the arrows in the Edit Clef window.

6 Click OK, and the part should now be displayed correctly.

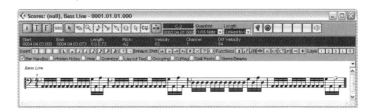

❖ Close the Score editor.

For hard core number crunchers, the List editor provides a detailed list of all the MIDI events making up a part.

❖ Select the Bass Line part again, and select "MIDI > Open List Editor" or press [ctrl][G].

The List editor is split into three main sections from left to right. The main event list details precisely each MIDI event in the part, such as the notes. The grid section shows the time and length of each MIDI event. The last section shows a value depending on the type of MIDI event; in the case of a note, the lengths of these horizontal bars represent note velocity.

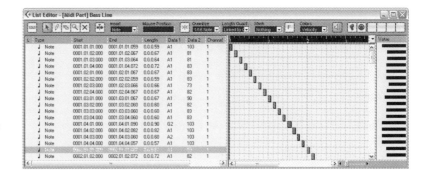

❖ Close the List editor.

The final MIDI editor offered by Cubase is the Drum editor, which, as the name suggests, is ideal for editing drum parts.

❖ Select one of the Drum Loop parts and select "MIDI > Open Drum Editor."

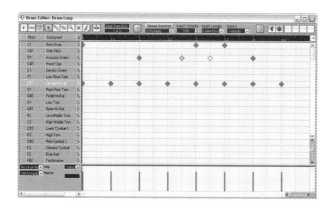

The Drum editor is divided into a series of horizontal rows. Each row is dedicated to a single drum sound, and any notes to be played by that row are shown as diamonds.

❖ Close the Drum editor.

Setting the Default Editor

Although the Key editor opens by default when you double-click a part, it's possible to change this and choose your own default editor.

1 Select "File > Preferences."

2 Select the "Event Display > MIDI" panel.

3 Choose your default editor from the Default Edit Action pop-up menu and click OK.

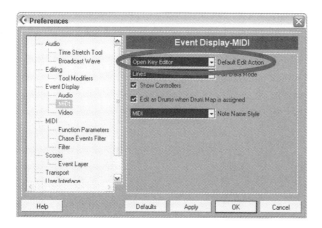

The Audio Editors

It's vital to remember the difference between audio parts and audio events when accessing the audio editors. Simply put, an audio part contains one or more audio events, and audio you record or import into Cubase, for example, will be displayed on the Project window as audio events. In fact, audio in Cubase will be an audio event unless you've specifically turned it into a part for editing purposes. Audio parts can be a useful way of grouping together events that should stay together, like the distorted guitar part at bar 1, and we'll look at an example of this in the next chapter.

To create an audio part, select one or more audio events in the Project window and select "Audio > Events to Part."

To convert an audio part back into one or more audio events, select the audio part and then select "Audio > Dissolve Part."

One of Cubase's strong points is the level of audio editing that's possible without leaving the Project window. However, when you want to carry out a finer degree of audio editing, Cubase provides two audio editing windows to meet your needs.

When you double-click on an audio part, such as the distorted guitar part at bar 1, Cubase opens the Audio Part Editor, as displayed below. This looks (and works) like the Project window and is useful when compiling the perfect take from different audio events, for example.

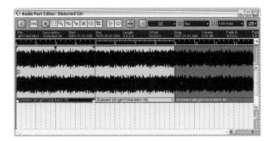

Double-clicking an audio event in the Audio Part editor or the Project window opens the Sample Editor. This allows you to edit the actual audio files making up your song, just like you would in a sample editing application like WaveLab or Sound Forge, for example.

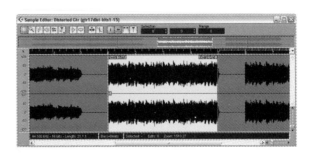

Learning to Arrange **3**

Now you're familiar with the basic aspects of Cubase, let's look at some arranging techniques with the aid of the demo song.

Moving Parts/Events

As we've already mentioned, the music you record into Cubase is displayed on the Project window as parts and events along a time ruler and various tracks. These parts and events can be moved around freely, allowing you to try out different ideas.

1 Try moving a part or event in the Project window by simply dragging it with the mouse.

When you move a part or event, notice how a pop-up box moves around with the mouse, showing you the location the part or event will be placed at when you release the mouse button.

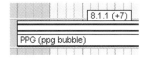

2 When you've moved a part, select "Edit > Undo" or press ctrl Z.

This command always takes you a step back in the list of actions you carry out on a song; so in this case, the part or event you moved is put back to its original location.

Understanding the Snap Function

When you move parts and events in the Project window, they automatically lock to a musical grid, which by default has a sixteenth note resolution. This behavior in Cubase is known as Snap mode and can be toggled with the Snap button on the toolbar.

Snap mode goes much further than simply switching it on or off, and there are three pop-up menus to configure the way that parts and events can be moved around on the Project window.

Snap   Grid   Quantize

For this guide we'll be using the default grid for Snap mode, so make sure the values for the pop-up menus are set the same as in the screenshot above.

❖ Snap should be set to Grid, and Grid should be set to Use Quantize.

The resolution of the musical grid that parts and events "snap" to can now be set with the Quantize menu. If you want parts to snap to quarter notes, select "1/4 Note" from the Quantize menu, for example.

❖ Set Quantize to "1/1 Note," which will make parts and events snap to whole bar positions.

Moving Many Parts Simultaneously

Just like moving files around in the Windows Explorer, multiple parts and events can be dragged around in the

Project window by drawing a box around them. You can also shift-click parts events manually to make multiple selections, and if you want to select every part and event in the Project window, select "Edit > Select > All" or press ctrl A.

Let's create some space at the beginning of the demo song to add an eight-bar introduction:

1 Press ctrl A to select all the parts and events in the Arrange window.

2 Move the selection to bar 9 by dragging any one of the selected parts.

3 Click in an empty section of the Project window to de-select the current selection. Remembering to deselect parts and events helps to prevent accidentally moving or deleting them.

Copying Parts and Events

To copy parts and events in the Project window, simply hold down alt while you drag the selection, as if you were moving the parts and events.

We want to copy a part from the end of the song to use it as the main part of our introduction:

1 Scroll the song along to bar 41 and locate the "Clean Guitar (clean arp)" event.

2 Hold down alt and drag this event to bar 1 on the same track.

3 Now copy the same event to bar 21 on the same track.

4 Locate the "PPG (ppg bubble)" event at bar 9 and copy it to bar 29 on the same track.

5 Copy the first Bass Line part at bar 9 to bar 33 on the same track.

6 Copy the Bass Line part at bar 17 to bars 19, 37 and 39 on the same track.

Introducing the Pool

A list of all audio events used in a song is stored in what's known as the Pool. Audio files can be imported into the Pool and dragged into your arrangement, but for this example the Pool already contains some files for you to add to the Project window.

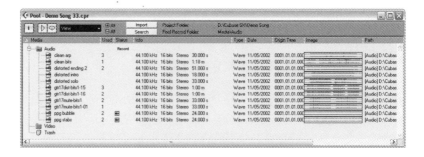

1 Open the Pool by selecting "Project > Pool" or by pressing $\boxed{ctrl}\boxed{P}$.

2 Locate and drag the "distorted intro" event onto the Distorted Solo track at position 4.1.1 in the Project window. You may need to move the Pool and Project windows around on your screen in order to make this possible.

3 If the Pool window vanishes behind the Project window, simply press ⌈ctrl⌉⌈P⌉ again.

4 Locate the "distorted solo" event and drag it onto the Distorted Solo track at position 12.1.1 in the Project window. Again, you may need to scroll the Project window or reorganize your screen to do this.

5 Close the Pool window.

Merging Parts/Events

Sometimes it can be useful to join many parts or events into one part. For example, our demo song consists of mainly four bar blocks, yet the drum track is made from a single one-bar part copied several times. So let's convert the eight one-bar drum parts into two four-bar drum parts.

1 Select the glue tool from the toolbar.

2 Click the first drum part at bar 9—notice how it becomes merged with the next part along.

You can also select the glue tool by pressing ⌈4⌉ on the main computer keyboard—but not the numeric keypad.

3 Click the first part again and the same thing happens.

4 Click the first part again and it now becomes a four-bar drum part.

5 Do the same thing with the drum part at bar 13.

You can also select the arrow tool by pressing ⑦ on the main computer keyboard.

6 Select the arrow tool again by clicking on the Objection Selection icon on the toolbar.

Copying Multiple Parts/Events

If you've played the demo song through, you might notice that the drums seem to stop rather abruptly, so let's make some copies of our new four-bar drum part throughout the whole song. While we could copy the part manually by dragging with [alt] held down as before, there's a quicker way to make multiple copies.

1 Select one of the four-bar drum parts.

A neat way of setting the locators is to place the Project Cursor where you want a locator and press [ctrl]⑦ or [ctrl]② to set the left or right locator to that position respectively.

2 Set the left locator to bar 17.

3 Set the right locator to bar 51.

4 Select "Edit > Fill Loop."

The space between the left and right locators is filled with copies of the drum part, and notice that the last part is truncated by two bars so that the space is filled exactly.

Deleting Parts/Events

Removing parts and events from the Project window is fairly simple.

1 Select one or more parts and events to be deleted.

2 Press the backspace key ⌫.

When audio events and parts are deleted in this way, it's important to remember that they are not deleted from your hard disk as well. See the FAQ from page 58 onwards for advice on cleaning up your hard disk.

1 Delete the extra two-bar drum part at bar 49.

2 Delete the drum part at bar 29.

Cutting Up Parts/Events

Sometimes you may only want to remove small chunks from an event or part, rather than deleting the whole thing. Let's say, for example, we want to remove some half-bar sections from the distorted guitar part at bar 33 to create a little musical variation.

1 Select the scissors tool on the toolbar.

2 Notice how the scissors tool snaps to the whole bar grid as you move it around the project window.

3 Because we want to chop half-bar sections, change the Quantize value to "1/2 Note."

4 Click along the distorted guitar part at bar 33 and cut it into half bar events.

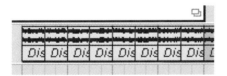

Muting Parts/Events

We've already looked at how to delete parts and events, but sometimes you might want to try out new arrangement ideas without actually removing the parts and events from the Project window. In these cases, it can be useful to mute the parts instead.

1 Select the mute tool from the toolbar.

2 Mute the second half of every bar.

3 Play the song from around bars 32 to 38 to hear the result.

4 I think it sounds better with the last distorted guitar half-bar section playing, so click it again to unmute it.

If you like this new aspect to the song (and for the sake of this tutorial, let's pretend you do!), turn these chopped up distorted guitar events into a single part.

1 Draw a box around the eight distorted guitar events to select them.

2 Select "Audio > Events to Part."

Basic Mixing

One of the most amazing aspects in Cubase is that you can run an entire studio from inside your computer with no extra hardware, aside from a MIDI keyboard and a soundcard of course. The Track Mixer that we briefly looked at earlier, for example, gives you a fully functional mixing desk to produce the overall sound of the audio and MIDI tracks on the Project window.

1 Open the file Demo Song 3.cpr from the Demo Song folder you copied to your hard drive.

2 Press F3 to open the Track Mixer.

Understanding the Track Mixer

The Track Mixer can be configured in many different ways to show you exactly what you want to see. The two main views are known as Normal and Extended.

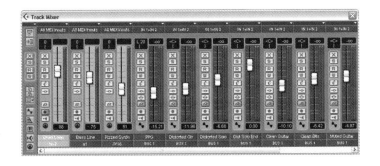

The Normal view in the Track Mixer.

The Extended view in the Track Mixer.

Notice how both audio and MIDI tracks are shown in the Track Mixer. Audio tracks have a dark blue background behind the fader, while MIDI tracks have a lighter beige background behind the fader.

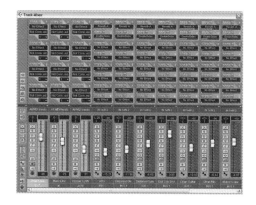

❖ You can switch between the Normal and Extended mixer views by clicking the Extended/Normal mixer view button on the Common panel, which is the left-hand strip of the Track Mixer.

You can decide what's displayed in the Extended view by selecting from the Global View pop-up menu (in the Common panel), or each of the Channel View pop-up menus. In this way, you can display the same extended controls for every channel strip on the mixer, or different extended controls for individual channels.

Click here for the Global View pop-up menu

Click here for a Channel View pop-up menu

An extended view pop-up menu

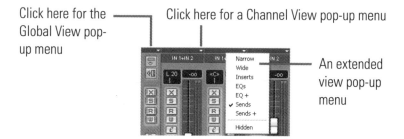

If you're running out of space to display all the channel strips on your screen horizontally, you can set all the channels to a Narrow view by selecting Narrow from the Global View pop-up menu. You can also select specific channels to be displayed as Narrow by selecting Narrow from the Channel View pop-up menu on those channels.

The Basic Channel Strip Controls

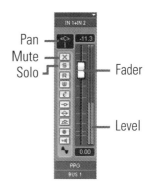

Pan
Mute
Solo
Fader
Level

The main fader on each channel strip controls the volume for that track, and the output level is shown by the level meter. The pan control sets the position of the track in the stereo image (from left to right).

> Dragging the volume fader or pan control with *shift* held down allows you to make finer adjustments.

The default value for a volume fader is 0dB (decibels), meaning that the level of the signal stays the same—nothing is added or taken away. You can *ctrl*-click any fader or control to reset it to the default value, so *ctrl*-clicking a volume fader resets it to 0dB, while a pan control will be reset to the center position.

Mute and Solo

If you want to hear one track in isolation from the rest of the music, click the channel Solo button for that track. When you play the song now, only the track with the Solo button active will be heard until you disable the Solo button again. In the same way, you can activate a track's Mute button to hear everything but the muted track. The track won't be heard again until you disable the Mute button.

It's also possible to "solo" many tracks simultaneously, which can be useful if you want to hear only the drum and bass tracks, for example. And again, in the same way, you can mute multiple tracks. So if you want to hear everything except the drum and bass tracks, simply click the Mute button on both tracks.

You can also find duplicate Mute and Solo buttons on the tracks themselves in the Project window. And, in addition to Mute and Solo buttons, the Inspector also contains duplicate volume and pan controls.

The Master Channel

The Master Channel

The channels on the mixer get mixed down to a master stereo pair, and you can see this on the Track Mixer by activating the Master button on the Common panel.

Hide/Show the Master Channel

A Word or Two about Digital Mixing

At its most basic, the point of mixing is to achieve a good balance of all the tracks, making sure that everything can be heard and nothing is distorting or overloading. The level meters are useful, but they're not a substitute for your ears.

While it's true that digital mixing systems like the Track Mixer in Cubase are less forgiving than their analog counterparts, it's surprising how far they can be pushed. If the level meter for a channel is showing red, always solo that channel and check the sound isn't distorting, pulling the fader down if necessary. The trick is to keep the master fader at 0dB while moving the channel faders to ensure the master levels don't overload.

Insert and Send Effects

Effects are used to add some sonic spice to your music production, making certain sounds more distinctive and interesting to the listener.

There are two ways an effect can be used: as a "send" effect, or as an "insert." When a send effect is used, a proportion of the signal is sent to the effect and the *wet* output from the effect gets mixed with the original *dry* signal. When an insert effect is used, the whole signal goes through the effect so you're left with only the wet output.

A *wet* signal refers to one that contains some processing by an effect; a *dry* signal is one that doesn't.

Although there are no strict rules about which types of effects should be used as sends or inserts, there are some general guidelines worth following:

An important point, especially when it comes to computer resources, is that send effects can be used globally by all audio tracks, whereas insert effects can only apply to one particular audio track.

❖ Sound transformation plug-ins such as dynamics (compressors, limiters, expanders and gates), EQs and filters should be run as inserts.

❖ Reverb is almost always used as a send effect.

❖ Delay and modulation effects are commonly used in both insert and send positions. Chorus and delay are often used as sends, while flangers and phasers find their place as inserts.

Using Send Effects

To add some reverb to our demo song mix, we need to set up a reverb plug-in as a send effect.

1 Open the VST Send Effects window by selecting "Devices > VST Send Effects," or by pressing F6.

2 Click the "No Effect" label on the first empty rack space and select "Reverb > Reverb A" from the pop-up menu, which lists all of the installed plug-ins.

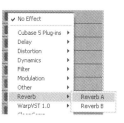

power button (on by default)

output volume of the effect

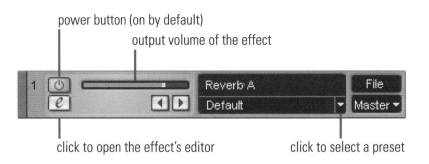

click to open the effect's editor   click to select a preset

With the reverb effect ready for action in our virtual effects rack, the next step is to send signals from the Track Mixer to the effect.

1 Open the Track Mixer. (Quick reminder: press [F3].)

2 Make sure the extended mixer view is activated.

3 Locate the "Clean Guitar" track and click the white triangle in the black strip just above the input selector.

4 Select "Sends" from the Channel View pop-up menu for that channel.

5 There are eight sends available, and Cubase automatically patches these controls to the effects set up in the VST Send Effects window—notice that the first send control is labelled "Reverb A," the plug-in we just selected.

6 Activate the first send by clicking the power-plug-styled button.

7 Drag the slider underneath the "Reverb A" label to set how much of the "Clean Guitar" signal is sent to the reverb effect.

It's important to have the song playing when you're tweaking effects settings so you can hear exactly how your changes affect the overall mix. Sometimes it can be useful to solo the track you're applying effects so you can hear how the sound of that one track is affected.

❖ With the song playing, try adding the reverb effect to other tracks in the same way we just added it to the Clean Guitar track.

❖ When you're happy with the general idea of using send effects, try adding the "Delay > DoubleDelay" effect to slot two in the VST Send Effects window, and apply this to various tracks.

Using Insert Effects

Now you know how to use send effects, adding an insert effect to a channel is actually much easier. Let's add the Phaser effect as an insert to the Clean Guitar track.

1 Make sure the Track Mixer is open and the extended mixer view is activated.

2 Locate the Clean Guitar track and click the white triangle in the black strip just above the input selector.

3 Select "Inserts" from the Channel View pop-up menu for that channel.

4 There are eight inserts available, and the signal flows from the top down, passing through all the effect slots from one to eight.

5 In the first insert slot on the Clean Guitar track, click the "No Effect" label and select "Modulation > Phaser."

6 The effect is automatically activated and its editor window is opened.

7 Make any adjustments and then close the window.

Recording Your First Song

5

Now you've mastered the basics of arranging and mixing, let's take those skills further and start recording a song from scratch. In this chapter we'll look at setting up a new song, recording an audio track, and then programming a drum part using a VST instrument.

Creating a New Project

To start a new project in Cubase:

The New Project dialog offers many template projects with different configurations to act as a starting point, saving you from having to start from scratch each time.

You may want to investigate creating templates with the "File > Save As Template" command for your own studio setup.

1 Select "File > New Project" or press *ctrl* *N*.

2 Select "Empty" and click OK.

This will provide an empty Project window so we can look at all the steps needed to set-up a new song.

3 Select a folder to be used as the project folder for the new song from the Select directory window.

4 Click OK and a new empty Project window will be displayed.

5 Because a Cubase project file is not created automatically, it's a good idea to save a project file before we go any further.

> Cubase project files have the *.cpr file extension.

6 Select "File > Save As" or press [ctrl][S].

7 In the file selector, make sure you save the project file within the correct project folder, type in a name for your project and click Save. While you don't have to store your project files in the project folder, it makes sense to keep everything in one place.

Now we're ready to start setting up the song.

A project folder is where Cubase saves the information for your project, including audio files you import or record, any edits, and so on.

Creating and Recording an Audio Track

Before we can do anything else, an audio track needs to be created in our project.

1 Right-click on the track list and select "Add Audio Track" from the pop-up menu.

2 Rename the track by double-clicking its name in the track list, typing something suitable and then pressing [↵].

Setting Up the Inputs

The next step is to make sure you can get audio from your soundcard into Cubase, and first of all you need to check the correct audio inputs are activated in the VST Inputs window.

1 Select "Devices > VST Inputs" or press F5 to open the VST Inputs window.

The number of inputs shown in the VST Inputs window depends on how many physical audio inputs your soundcard has. If you're using the standard soundcard on your computer, you'll probably only have one stereo input pair.

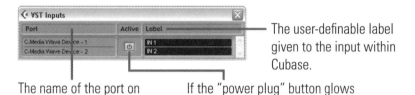

The user-definable label given to the input within Cubase.

The name of the port on your audio hardware, as set by the manufacturer.

If the "power plug" button glows blue, that pair of stereo inputs is active.

With a more advanced soundcard featuring multiple inputs, you may have more stereo input pairs available. If you don't see all the inputs you're expecting in the window, check that you have the correct ASIO driver selected (as explained in the first chapter) and consult your soundcard's manual.

2 Activate the inputs you'll be recording into by clicking the "power plug" buttons in the Active column to enable and disable the inputs as required.

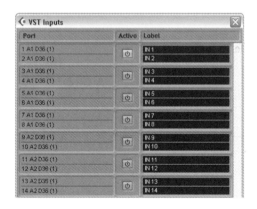

If you have a system with more than one stereo pair of inputs, only activate the input pairs you're actually going to be using. Each active input requires a small amount of valuable processing power.

Renaming the Input Labels

The names assigned to the inputs by default aren't particularly meaningful, so it's a good idea to give them more appropriate labels. This is especially true if you have multiple inputs that stay connected to the same gear in your studio, such as mics, keyboards, guitars, and so on. To rename an input:

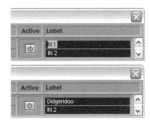

1 Click the label of the input you want to rename.

2 Type in a new name.

3 Press ↵.

With the inputs activated and labeled, we're ready to assign an input to our audio track.

Assigning the Inputs

Assigning audio inputs to audio tracks is where you say to Cubase, "I want my mic, which is plugged into this input on my audio hardware, to be recorded on this track in my project." To do this:

1 Open the Track Mixer. (Quick reminder, press F3.)

2 Just above the volume fader and pan control on the audio channel is the input selector.

> The input selector shows which input is routed to that particular audio track, and when you have a project with multiple audio tracks, they can each be assigned to different inputs.

3 If it isn't showing the correct input (i.e. where you want to record from), click the input selector and choose the input you want from the pop-up menu.

Monitoring

Monitoring is the term given for listening to an audio signal being played live, usually before and during the recording process. Follow the instructions below, depending on what audio hardware you're using, and then proceed to the "Getting the Right Level" section.

I'm Using Extra Audio Hardware with It's Own ASIO Driver

Soundcards and other audio devices that come with dedicated ASIO drivers are usually capable of low enough latencies to monitor directly through Cubase, which is the best possible scenario.

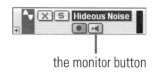

the monitor button

If Direct Monitoring is unavailable, it means that your ASIO driver doesn't support this feature. Consult the manufacturer of your audio hardware about ASIO 2 drivers.

❖ Enable the monitor button on the audio track and you should be able to hear the input of the signal you're going to record routed through the Track Mixer.

If you perceive any latency, try the following:

1 Reduce the buffer size on the audio hardware as described on page 12.

2 Open the VST Multitrack panel on the Device Setup window and activate Direct Monitoring.

I'm Using the Standard Audio Hardware

In an ideal world you'd want to monitor what you're recording through the device that's actually making the recording—in this case, the computer running Cubase. However, because most general computer soundcards aren't optimized for professional audio, this type of monitoring isn't usually possible.

The problem is that we need to hear what's coming from Cubase (whether it's the metronome click now, or a backing track later on) mixed with the instrument that we're recording. Listening to what we're recording is easy, and listening to what's coming from Cubase is easy. However, without some way of mixing the two together we can't listen to both at the same time, and this is unfortunately what we need to do.

You could buy a little mixer to do the job, but there's also a neat little trick you might be able to try with your soundcard.

1 Open the Windows Volume Control. If you're not sure how to do this, look in the online Windows help for "Volume Control" and you'll find the directions.

2 Notice that the inputs (such as Microphone and Line In) are muted by default.

3 Uncheck the mute control for the input your instrument is plugged into on the soundcard.

You should now be able to hear your input mixed with the output of Cubase without having to make any other changes or buy any extra hardware. Just remember to mute the input again after you've finished recording.

If you can't see your soundcard's inputs in the Windows Volume Control:

1. Select "Options > Properties."
2. Make sure all the check boxes are ticked in the "Show the following volume controls" panel.
3. Click OK.

the record button

If you have some audio recorded on a track and during playback the level meter seems to be dead (or shows incorrect readings for what you're hearing), the record button is probably active and is showing the level of the input—not the output signal.

Getting the Right Level

With the monitoring sorted out, make sure the record button is activated (highlighted red) on the audio track we're going to record on. You can activate the record button by simply clicking it, although by default Cubase always activates the record button on the selected track.

When the record button is activated, the level meter on that track shows the input signal, and you should use this reading to set the record level on your instrument. The level meter should light up to about 90%, and even if the audio you're recording is quiet in the final mix, it should always be recorded as loudly as possible to maintain the highest signal quality.

❖ The volume faders on the Track Mixer control the level of the audio output only—you can't use them to boost the level of the signal you're recording. Any input level increases have to be carried out at source.

The Tempo and the Metronome

It's essential to record with a metronome click set to the correct tempo—if you don't, it will be almost impossible to edit the audio properly at a later stage.

We're almost ready to record, but before this happens you need to set the correct tempo, make sure you can hear the metronome click, and decide what you want for the count-in.

1 Make sure the Master button is disabled on the Transport Panel. If the Master button is highlighted in blue, click it to disable the Tempo track.

> The Tempo track is a 'hidden' track that controls tempo and time signature changes within a song. However, at this stage you won't need to worry about it.

2 Double-click the tempo value on the transport bar, type in a new value and press ⏎.

3 Play the song with the metronome click to check whether the tempo is appropriate.

4 If you can't hear the metronome click, check that the Click button is active (highlighted blue) on the Transport Panel. If it isn't, click the Click button to activate it, or press Ⓒ.

You can configure the sound of the metronome in the Metronome Setup window.

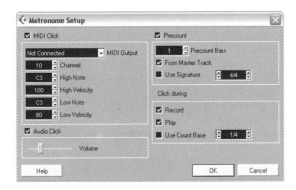

❖ Open the Metronome Setup window by selecting "Transport > Metronome Setup" or by ⒸⓉⓇⓁ-clicking the Click button on the Transport Panel.

The audio click is useful when you're not using an external MIDI sound source, so if you can't hear the click when the Audio Click parameter is disabled, you'll need to make sure it's activated. However, if you have an external MIDI sound source, or your soundcard has onboard sounds, try using the MIDI Click settings instead of the rather shrill audio alternative.

Setting the Count-in

The count-in is known in Cubase-speak as the pre-count.

A count-in is the number of bars Cubase plays from the point you press the Record button to when the recording actually begins. By default, when you press Record you'll hear the metronome click for one bar on its own, and then the recording will commence. You can specify how many bars the count-in lasts for with the Precount Bars parameter in the Metronome Setup window.

❖ Close the Metronome Setup window.

Recording the First Track

After all the preflight checks are complete, it's time to begin the take-off procedure and press the red button to start recording your musical masterpiece.

1 Make sure "Transport > Start Record at Left Locator" is selected.

> This option does what it says. It means that when you press record, the recording will always begin from the position of the left locator, and not the Project Cursor. This is especially useful when you want to have several attempts at the same section.

2 Set the left locator to the position you want to start recording from, which will probably be bar 1.

> The quickest way of doing this is to click once in the upper part of the time ruler at the position you want to set the locator to. This sets both the left and right locator to that position.

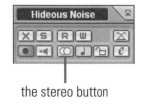

the stereo button

3 If you want to record in stereo, make sure the stereo button for that track (which is located on the Inspector) is activated.

4 Click the Record button on either the Transport Panel or the Project window, or press ⊡ on the numeric keypad.

5 Click the Stop button on either the Transport Panel or Project window, or press ⍰ on the numeric keypad when you want to end the recording.

6 You can now play the recording back and pat yourself on the back if you're happy with it. If not, select "Edit > Undo Record", or press ⍰⍰, and try again.

If you can't hear what you've just recorded when you play the song back, check the monitor button is disabled.

And that's all there is to recording an audio track!

Getting a Handle on Parts and Events

One thing you might have noticed about the appearance of parts and events is that they contain "handles" on either side. The lower corner handles are used for adjusting the start and end points of the part or event, so if you've recorded an eight-bar section and it's shown as being nine bars in length, simply pull back the right side of the part or event using the lower corner handle. You can adjust the starting point of a part or event by dragging the lower left corner handle on the part or event.

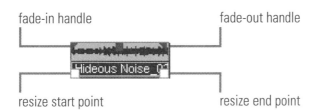

fade-in handle   fade-out handle

Hideous Noise

resize start point   resize end point

In addition to being able to adjust the start and end points, for audio events you can also drag out fade-ins and -outs.

Programming a Drum Track

Another common task when producing a song in Cubase is to program a MIDI drum track, so that's exactly what we're going to do next.

Setting Up a VST Instrument

Instead of using any extra equipment, we'll use a VST instrument within Cubase to produce the drum sounds.

1 Select "Devices > VST Instruments" or press F11 to open the VST Instruments window.

2 Click the "No VST Instrument" label in the first slot and select "Drums > lm-7"—the LM-7 is a virtual drum machine.

3 Open the Track Mixer.

> VST Instrument channels have a green background behind the faders.

4 Notice how Cubase automatically patches the VST instrument into its own channel on the Track Mixer. VST instrument channels work just like audio channels, and you can use send and insert effects in exactly the same way.

Preparing a MIDI Track

1 Create a new MIDI track on the Project window by right-clicking in an empty area of the track list and selecting "Add MIDI Track" from the pop-up menu.

2 Double-click the new track's name in the track list and call it something original, like "Drums" for instance.

3 With the new track selected, in the Inspector set "out:"
to "out: lm-7" by clicking on it and selecting "lm-7"
from the pop-up menu.

> This routes the output of the MIDI track to the LM-7 VST instrument.

Creating and Programming the Drum Part

In order to program some drums onto our drum track,
we need to create an empty MIDI part.

1 Select the pencil tool from the toolbar.

2 Drag from bar 1 to bar 3 on the Drums track to create a
new two-bar MIDI part.

3 Select the arrow tool again.

With a MIDI track prepared and a MIDI part created,
we're ready to enter some notes.

1 Select the drum part we just created.

2 It can be really useful to have Cubase playing in cycle
mode when you're programming parts, so set the locators to the start and end points of the drum part, bar 1
and bar 3. You can do this by simply selecting "Transport > Locators to Selection" or by pressing P.

3 Make sure the Project Cursor is between the locators
and start the song playing.

4 Select "MIDI > Open Drum Editor." You can program
MIDI parts using any of the MIDI editors, but the
drum editor is, unsurprisingly, the easiest one to use
for programming drums.

5 Make sure the drum editor is scrolled to the top, so you can see the "Bass Drum" track at the top of the editor.

6 Select the drum stick tool.

7 Using the drum stick tool, click on the grid where you want to enter drum notes. Adding notes along the "Bass Drum" track, for example, will cause those notes to be played by the bass drum.

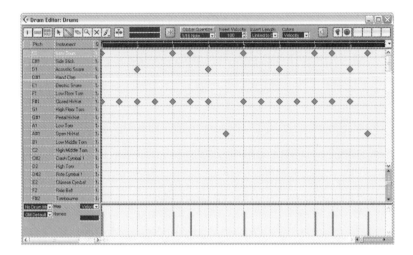

8 To remove drum notes, simply click them again with the drum stick tool. You can also select the eraser tool and click the notes you want to erase.

9 When you've finished entering notes and you've got the part sounding just right, close the editor and stop the song playing.

10 For information about copying parts on the Project window, you might want to take another look at pages 25 and 28.

Recording MIDI Tracks

Now you know how to record an audio track and work with VST instruments, recording a MIDI track should be a piece of cake. Assuming the red MIDI input indicator flashes on the Transport Panel when you play notes on your MIDI keyboard (this was discussed in the first chapter), you're ready to go.

1 Add a MIDI track to the Project window.

2 Set-up a VST instrument (if you don't have an external MIDI sound source you want to use)—the A1 and JX16 synths bundled with Cubase are both excellent for recording keyboard parts.

3 Set the output of the MIDI track to your MIDI sound source, via the Inspector on the Project window.

4 Make sure the tempo, metronome and count-in are configured appropriately, exactly as described for recording audio tracks earlier in this chapter.

5 Click the Record button on the MIDI track if it isn't already highlighted.

6 Set the locators to the position you want to start recording from by clicking in the upper part of the time ruler.

7 Press Record when you're ready, and Stop when you've finished.

8 You can adjust the start and end points of the part with the handles, or edit it in more detail by double-clicking the part.

Mastering to CD or MP3

6

The final stage once you've recorded and mixed the music is known as mastering, and Cubase makes it possible to produce a Wave file you can burn directly to an audio CD, or an MP3 file you can upload to the Internet. In this chapter we're going to "master" the demo song.

❖ Open the file Demo Song 2.cpr.

Using Master Effects

In addition to the insert and send effects you patch into the audio channels on the Track Mixer, Cubase also provides a VST Master Effects window. This allows you to put up to eight extra insert effects on the master stereo output, enabling you to add dynamic processing to the overall mix, for example, to give your music that extra polish.

❖ Select "Devices > VST Master Effects" or press *F7* to open the VST Master Effects window.

The VST Master Effects window works in a similar way to the VST Send Effects window we looked at before, so let's add some common mastering effects to the demo song.

1 Click the "No Effect" label in slot seven and select "Dynamics > VSTDynamics" from the pop-up menu.

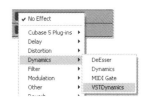

> Notice the blue "Master Gain" box between slots six and seven: this indicates that any effects in slots one to six will be processed before the volume fader on the master channel, and any effects in slots seven and eight will be processed after the master volume fader.

2 If the VSTDynamics editor window doesn't open automatically, click the "e" button in slot seven.

3 We can make the overall mix sound more punchy by adding a little compression, so click the COMPRESSOR button to activate compression.

4 With the song playing over a fairly loud section, say from bar 9, start increasing the MakeUpGain control on the compressor and set it to about 8.0dB.

5 Because we've added a fair amount of volume to our final mix, you have to be especially careful not to overload the stereo outputs. To help us prevent this, click the LIMITER button to activate the limiter.

6 Set the Threshold of the limiter to −0.5dB, which means that no matter what goes into the limiter, nothing will come out louder than −0.5dB. This is why it's called a limiter!

7 With the song playing from around bar 9 again, try toggling the power-plug-styled button at the top of the VSTDynamics editor window to bypass the mastering effect. Even with relatively little effort, you can hear the difference that mastering can make to your music.

A Bit of Dither

Dithering is useful in Cubase because the internal mixing and effects are processed at 32-bit, even if your files and audio hardware is only 16-bit. Normally Cubase simply truncates the last 16 bits to get a 16-bit signal, so by using a dither plug-in, a small amount of low-level noise is added to smoothly round the 32 bits down to 16.

When exporting a final master file out of Cubase, it's advisable to use a plug-in that provides dithering, which is the process of getting digital audio from a high resolution to a low resolution while trying to keep as much of the dynamic range as possible.

❖ Dithering should always be the last process your audio goes through before reaching the output, so always use slot eight for your dithering plug-in.

❖ In the VST Master Effects window, click the "No Effects" label in slot eight and choose "Other > uv22hr."

> Note that by default it's set for dithering down to 16 bits.

Also Available on the Track Mixer

It's worth mentioning that the master effects are also accessible from the Extended view of the Track Mixer when the Master channel is active. This section looks and functions just like the insert effects on normal channels.

Open VST Master Effects window

Bypass master effects

The two buttons above the master fader allow you to open the VST Master Effects window, and bypass all eight master effects. This second button can be useful if you want to do quick comparisons without having to click the power button for each master effect manually.

Exporting Your Stereo Master File

Once you're happy with the sound of any mastering plug-ins, it's time to export the audio.

1 Set the left locator to the start of the song, which in this case is bar 1.

> The left locator sets where the export audio process will begin from.

2 Set the right locator to the end of the song—bar 51.

> The right locator sets the point where the export process ends, so it's important to listen carefully to the end of your song and make sure that any reverb tails aren't cut off. In other words, wait for a second or two of silence at the end of your song before placing the right locator.

A neat way of setting the locators is to place the Song Position Pointer where you want a locator and press `ctrl`+`1` or `ctrl`+`2` to set the left or right locator to that position respectively.

3 Select "File > Export > Audio Mixdown."

4 Set a location for the audio file and type in a name.

5 Set the Files of Type parameter to "Wave File" if you're creating a file to burn to an audio CD, or "MPEG Layer 3 File" if you're creating an MP3 file.

6 For MP3 files, set Channels to Stereo, Sample Rate to "44.100kHz," and Attributes to "128 kBit/s; 44.100kHz; Stereo." These are the most common settings for MP3 files, but feel free to experiment.

> You can enter additional information for the MP3 file, such as the song title, artist name and so on by clicking the Options button.

7 For Wave files, set Channels to "Stereo Interleaved," Resolution to "16 Bit" and Sample Rate to "44.100kHz." Disable Pool and Audio Track in the Import to group.

8 Make sure Automation and Effects are ticked in the Include group.

9 Click Save.

Troubleshooting

The biggest source of problems when using a powerful application like Cubase is running out of computer resources. With the whole studio being created in software, it's inevitable that the moment will come when the system simply runs out of gas and you start experiencing some problems. However, there are often ways to overcome these issues, and a useful starting point is to monitor the system performance.

❖ Select "Devices > VST Performance" or press F12 to open the VST Performance window.

The top meter indicates the load on your computer's processor—if the red light starts to flash, you're trying to do more than the processor can handle. The bottom meter shows the performance of your disk drives, and playing a large number of tracks simultaneously can put a fair amount of pressure on your storage device. So if the red light starts to flash, Cubase is unable to read all the data it needs from the disk.

Saving Processor Power

The basic audio functions like mixing don't really put too much strain on your computer—the big killer in terms of processor drains is running a number of plug-in effects and instruments. If the CPU meter is overloading and the song no longer plays back without glitches, you have two options: either turn the plug-ins off, or start bouncing the tracks containing insert effects, or the audio output of VST instruments.

The process of bouncing is just like preparing files for CD burning, which we looked at in the last chapter, except you don't need to use any mastering plug-ins. Simply solo the track to be bounced, set the left and right locators to encompass any music on the track, and export the audio. This time you'll want to select the "Import to Pool and Audio Track" options in the Export window.

If you have an audio track containing insert effects, this is a good candidate for bouncing. Once you've bounced the track, simply disable the insert effects and mute the track, leaving the new 'bounced' track playing instead.

Improving Your Disk Performance

It's unlikely that you'll run into disk-related performance problems if you have a fairly modern computer, since most drives are capable of playing an impressive number of audio tracks. However, if you do run into problems, try the following:

If you like reading computer specifications, hard drives for audio should be capable of at least 7200 RPM.

1 Check your disk for errors and defragment it.

2 Have a second hard drive in your computer for Cubase SX projects.

If you can't use another hard drive (or you're already using another hard drive), you'll have to start bouncing multiple tracks down to stereo submixes.

Consult Windows Help for information about hard drive maintenance if you're unsure about checking for errors or defragmenting.

FAQ

8

How do I install extra VST plug-in effects and instruments?

The procedure for installing VST plug-in effects and instruments is identical, and most of the time the plug-in will come with a simple installer program to take care of the process automatically. However, if there's no installer (which is often the case with non-commercial plug-ins), you can install them manually by copying the DLL and associated files to the C:\Program Files\Steinberg\VST Plugins\ folder.

> The drive letter C is used as it's the most common for system drives. If you can't find the folder on drive C, look on the drive where you installed Cubase.

❖ If you run into difficulties, always consult the documentation that came with the plug-in—even if it's only a small text file.

Is there an easier way to scroll around the Project window?

Yes. If your mouse has a scroll wheel/button, simply hold it down while the mouse pointer is in the main arranging area of the Project window. The pointer will change it's shape to a hand and you can now scroll both horizontally and vertically by moving the mouse until you release the button. Slightly cumbersome to explain, but impossible to live without once experienced.

When I delete an audio part or event from the Project window, does it get deleted from my hard disk?

No. Although the audio part or event is gone from the Project window, it will still be referenced in the project and remain on your hard drive.

❖ Open the Pool. (Quick reminder: press ⒸⓉⓇⓁ Ⓟ)

You'll notice that the Pool contains three folders: Audio, Video and Trash. When an audio event is no longer used on the Project window, Cubase automatically moves it to the Trash folder. And just like the Recycle Bin on the Windows desktop, you can "empty" the Trash folder in your Cubase project and delete the files from disk.

1 Select "Pool > Empty Trash."

If you don't want to remove every audio event in the Trash folder, simply drag the events you want to keep back into the Audio folder.

2 Click Erase. Clicking "Remove from Pool" removes the files from the Pool, but doesn't delete them from the disk.

Warning! Once you click Erase, the files will be permanently deleted and there's no way to retrieve them.

Sometimes when the song is playing, the Project window seems to get stuck and doesn't follow the Project Cursor. What can I do?

In order for the Project window to follow the Project Cursor during playback, you need to make sure Follow Mode is active on the Project window's toolbar.

You can also toggle Follow Mode by pressing Ⓕ.

CD-ROM Contents

On the CD-ROM included with this book, you'll find a collection of essential resources.

A Demo Version of Cubase SX

If you don't yet own a copy of Cubase SX and are using this guide to get more familiar with the package, this demo version will let you work through the tutorials without having to make any extra purchase.

The Demo Song Folder

This folder contains materials used in the tutorials and should be copied to your computer's hard drive.

A Collection of Freeware VST Plug-ins

The plug-in effects and instruments bundled with Cubase provide plenty of possibility, but we've included some of the best free plug-ins around for those of you who just can't get enough.

See the FAQ on page 58 for a guide to installing VST plug-ins, or check the instructions accompanying each software item on the CD-ROM.

Internet Links

10

The official site for Cubase is http://www.cubase.net/ and provides news, interviews and other features, plus a discussion forum to discuss your problems with the rest of the world—those relating to Cubase, of course.

Steinberg's full web presence is http://www.steinberg.net/ and provides product information, a knowledge base, upgrades and more.

A mailing list for Cubase users can be found at http://groups.yahoo.com/group/cubase and they also have a useful resource page at http://www.cubasefaq.com/.

Sound On Sound, one of the most regarded English-language music technology magazines, has a web site at http://www.sospubs.co.uk/, where a monthly Cubase Notes column provides ideas and techniques for getting the most out of Cubase. If you're not a subscriber, articles become publicly readable after several months, and doing a search with the text "Cubase Notes" should provide some useful information.

My own web site is http://www.markwherry.com/, and you can hear my own musical efforts with Cubase at http://www.mp3.com/markwherry.

Index